The Pocket Coach

From Moth To Social Butterfly

A no nonsense guide to socialising for those who really can't be arsed

Author: Shahilla Barok

ISBN: 978-1-5272-0517-8

Published by www.publishandprint.co.uk

First Edition

Dedication

This book has only become a reality thanks to the two beautiful individuals in my life.

My gorgeous, intelligent and feisty daughters Hanna and Harli.

Thank you for your unfaltering belief in me and my ability to succeed.

Thank you for being my biggest fans no matter what. You have encouraged me to follow my dreams, despite it being a completely irresponsible thing to do, considering I am the sole bread winner!

More than that; thank you for riding the biggest tide of our lives with me. If I didn't have you on my most difficult days these past three years, I'm not sure I would have made it. I now know that it's going to be OK; together we are invincible.

Contents

Hello, is it this you're looking for?

Hi, I am your pocket coach; I love the sound of that! I have put together a few Pocket Coach books to give you a swift, loving kick in the right direction to achieving what you want to be, do or have; your goals, dreams and aspirations.

This series is one of my many whimsical ideas that have actually come to fruition.

A no nonsense, practical guide to getting things done and moving you towards your desired destination. The focus of this book is to help you release the social butterfly that resides within. I have cut out the fluff... well most of it, you need some fluff in order to understand my strategies and suggestions; otherwise you'll probably think I'm some crazy person having a laugh at your expense and that's just not true.

I want to make absolutely sure that this book is for you, I don't want it to collect dust on your shelf in some dark corner of your home. This is not a story book it's a doing book, it's a guide, crisp and concise, but a guide nonetheless.

Are you the type that doesn't really want to expend too much energy socialising?

Would you rather do what moths do and hover around the light fitting unnoticed?

Hate reading long-winded, fluff filled self-help books?

Like people to get to the point as quickly as possible?

You know you can't away get away with the light-fitting scenario too often don't you?

If you answered YES to all or at least three of the above, then I am pleased to announce that this book is indeed for you.

Make no mistake, there is work ahead and it requires your commitment if you want to see, feel, achieve the success you are looking for.

How to use this little book

This book is a start to becoming better at socialising. It will serve as a point of reference whenever you need it. Start by reading through the whole book, and doing the suggested activities as you go along. Once you have digested the entire book and are on your way to achieving your goal, you can pop it on a shelf and refer to the bits you need, when you need them. A sound investment in my opinion; a word of warning, brace yourself for a quirky, sometimes extremely corny sense of humour throughout this book.

I have already stated that you need to be committed to make this work. As I'm not physically with you, I am making an exerted effort to be with you in spirit, make no mistake about that; I have exercises for you to do, some of these are lists of questions, these are important questions and I want you to take your time answering them... you are not in a race, slow and steady does it. Thinking through each question carefully and answering honestly and thoroughly is the way forward; it will give you a better chance of success.

Work through the book systematically the first time, you might want to do this more than once; I leave that up to you.

I have intentionally announced the gems and activities so you can find them easily when revisiting. It is also my way of ensuring you don't tell porkies about not seeing them; they need to be done for you to achieve your butterfly transformation.

The gems are additional bits of advice, instruction; resources for you. More commonly known as tips; I prefer to call mine gems and you'll agree once you start to use them.

The activity areas have spaces for you to write down your answers so you don't have to juggle with this book, a notebook and a pen… change takes work and I want to make this work as convenient and easy for you. I know you'll find a way of getting those activities done.

The most important thing for you to note is that you need to put pen to paper when completing the activities. There is a good neurological reason for this, if you want to know what the science behind that is, email me. Until such time, I need you to just trust me and do your activities the old fashioned way, no tech, even if you can touch type!

The questions posed in the activities may not at first look like much, but this is deep level work and there may be times you feel a little exhausted after doing an activity, this is all normal. You are getting a psychological and emotional workout.

Take time to think each question through, write down your answer and before moving on to the next question ask yourself if there's more to write on the current question. Challenge yourself; I am only with you in spirit so you will have to push yourself to empty out all that comes to mind when you read each question.

Just to let you know, I have chosen to use the female pronoun throughout the book, not because this book isn't for everyone (it really is), but because I'm a girl and I am drawing on my own experiences when writing this.

Having read and worked through the book once (or twice), you then have a point of reference whenever you need it, changing behaviours, perceptions, values and beliefs takes time so you'll need to keep coming back to it.

I have created an 'at a glance' recap for you at the end of this book whilst you practice the strategies and approaches suggested.

If you keep referring back to this book and utilise the 'at a glance' guide at the end, you'll start to master this socialising malarkey in no time. In fact I believe you'll get so good at it, you won't even need to think about it anymore!

That's my vision for you…
unconscious competence baby,
that's where you'll be at!

A confession that needs to be aired here; I think it's better for you and I to start our new relationship on a platform of complete honesty. I make terrible jokes and can sometimes be stern at points in the book, but it's only because I have your best interests at heart and want this to work for you!

I love singing and with that in mind, you may on the odd occasion, see a hidden musical reference, for example: the heading for chapter one. You may roll your eyes (you may be doing that now… who knows?); smirk *or* you could make it into an additional, interesting layer to the book and see how many you can find. You might even find some unintentional ones; that would be even more interesting!

Introvert or Nervous Socialiser?

I have many friends who are introverts; they are great company to be around, interesting, funny and engaging. This relationship of ours took a while to establish but it was certainly worth every moment.

It is assumed by many that introverts just lock themselves away and don't want to step over the threshold of their own front door… wrong!

Introverts find excessive socialising tiring and most would rather not do it for that reason. Many have also informed me that they are not anti- social; they just want to have interesting conversations if they are going to make the effort to socialise.

Or, could you be a social butterfly that hasn't had the courage or confidence to spread her wings yet? Perhaps nerves get the better of you? Maybe you worry about what others may think of you?

Alternatively, you may be a real social person, who just hasn't achieved the level of social competence you would like; you don't yet have the key to savvy socialising. Fear not, you will, after this read.

In this world of networking and being in the know with different groups of people, socialising is imperative, you really do have to do a certain amount to get on in life, work and business.

Now I'm not one for caring too much what others think of me, I got over that some years ago. However, I know it's important to socialise and make connections, it feels good; it feeds my soul. There is nothing better than meeting new people and learning about their interesting lives, the stories they have to tell and the things you can learn from them.

Gem: You can learn new things from everyone you meet; you just need to be open to it. I am always amazed at how much I learn from the delegates who attend my various training sessions… they are quite amazing, inspiring and interesting people.

If you are someone who is considered introvert by others or yourself, I want you to know I have met some incredibly socially apt individuals whom I would never have believed to be introvert… but they identified themselves as introverts; incredible! But also proof that anyone can be socially competent despite their internal make-up.

You and I both know, nothing comes without commitment and some work; if you are willing to apply both then this book is your very own coach in your pocket, it's actually my mini printed proxy, a bit like having me in your head instead of in your ear. The only difference being, you can shut the book and ignore me if I start to get on your last nerve… You *mustn't* do that though, this is your personal journey and you owe it to yourself to put up with me until you reach your desired goal.

When you first take on this feisty little coach in print, you might find it a bit challenging… I mean literally challenging. All I ask is that you keep at it; I am truly delivering value here so you need to take this expedition on wholeheartedly.

Start Here

Right! Let's get going.

Introvert, shy, socialite, extrovert; no matter which you are you need to know that we as human beings are social beings. We need social contact as part of our psychological and emotional wellbeing, how much you need will depend on who you are as a person (introverts need less than extroverts).

People have made this social malarkey into a career, ever heard of social entrepreneurs? Well it seems there's money to be made through socialising! A dream career for some, a nightmare career for others but it's out there as a career.

You never know who you'll meet at any point in your day, week, month, life; I like to be ready to enjoy each experience. There are so many interesting people out there; the intellects who find their joy in collecting information and sharing that with others, the eccentrics who are really comfortable being exactly who they are, the shy introverts who love an interesting conversation but may not always be able to initiate it and of course, the phantasmagorical, really out there people, unpredictable, scary and intriguing all at the same time.

I personally am a lot of extrovert with a dash of introvert. I love people and people watching. I love social events where I can meet, learn from others and have fun. The introvert in me does however, have days where I want nothing more than to shut my front door and relish in the privacy and comfort of my home, my sanctuary. I believe most of us have a bit of both in us at varying levels; these levels are dependent on our upbringing, experiences, values and beliefs that make us who we are.

What is socialising?

The dictionary definition is:

1. "Mix socially with others" interact, converse, mix, mingle…
2. "Make (someone) behave in a way that is acceptable to their society." (1)

You and I are focusing on definition number one. I don't think definition number two applies… We won't have any clones on my watch, you are unique and that's how we want to keep it, no conformists need apply!

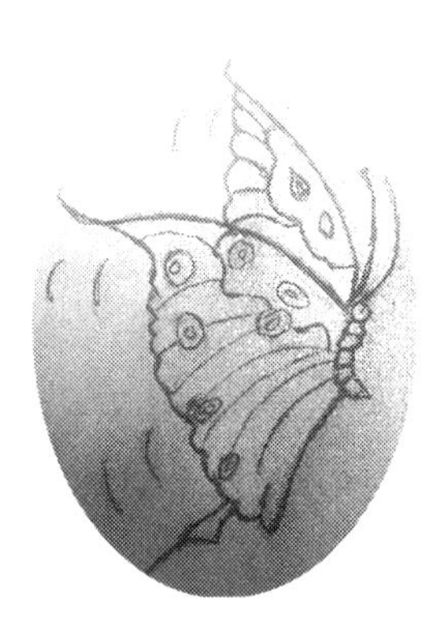

The definition of a social butterfly:

"A ***social butterfly*** *is someone who is* ***social*** *or friendly with everyone, flitting from person to person, the way a* ***butterfly*** *might. The word* ***social*** *comes from the Latin socius* ***meaning*** *'friend'. When you're being* ***social****, you're everyone's friend."* (2)

I like this definition, precise, to the point and it has taught me a bit of Latin at the same time!

This definition will have introverts cringing, feeling a bit nauseous and thinking "who wants to be everyone's friend?"

Actually, I'm no introvert but I'm thinking the same thing, however being able to speak with everyone in a social context is a great thing. This type of socialising is networking at its best, especially if you're looking for a career move, a promotion or you run your own business.

There are a couple more things I need to mention before we go any further.

1. **If you have social anxiety:**

"**Social anxiety** is the fear of interaction with other people that brings on self-consciousness, feelings of being negatively judged and evaluated, and, as a result, leads to avoidance." (3)

If your social anxiety is quite severe then this is not the right place for you to start. I would recommend you get some professional help; this book will be waiting on your shelf when you are ready to take the next step.

2. **Keep away from nasty fuckwits… unless you're up for some fun.**

A fuckwit, in this context is someone who decides they don't like you even before they have taken the time to get to know you.

We are quite amazing beings and one thing we don't make enough use of as amazing beings is our intuition.

I know you'll relate to this no matter whether you are an introvert or a nervous socialiser; this story will bring up the vision of one such incident in your life.

Note: **this is not fluff; it is a very important point from which you will learn something great.**

Imagine you are invited to a party by a good friend, however, you are aware that there are many people there you have never met before.

So you're suitably attired, looking fly and ready to roll. You make an appropriate entrance; whatever appropriate means to you (for me it's always later than I planned, but I have accepted that as my norm, as have my friends).

Your friend, the host greets and immediately does the 'host with the most' duty by introducing you to some people you haven't met before, you happily (is that too strong a word?) greet them, then you're introduced to someone that immediately makes you feel 'disliked' you know what I mean don't you? Your wonderful, dutiful intuition telling you…

"That person ain't no friend of yours honey, you keep away from that one!"

Does that resonate? Isn't our intuition so very clever and helpful?

So now you can relate to the described situation, I would like to announce that the unfriendly person described in my example scenario is the fuckwit.

Fuckwits are the people who feed their own ego at the expense of others. They are insecure in their own skin but display a hard, almost cruel confidence.

This fuckwit will know almost all the friends there, whether they get on with these friends is irrelevant, knowing more people than you in that context makes them feel powerful, superior. Their pleasure lies in making 'newcomers' feel insecure and intimidated, and you my dear, could become their next victim.

Fuckwits usually react this way toward people who reflect all the things they want to be but aren't... this is jealousy, envy, just plain nasty... call it what you want.

You have two choices, keep away or have some fun with it. On days where I am feeling 100% I go ahead and have some fun with the situation.

Which you choose depends on your gut instinct, don't ignore what your gut tells you, seriously, it's there to protect you. How you deal with it will depend on what your gut tells you and how you are feeling. Decide your approach based on your own resilience levels (you know yourself better than anybody).

The way you deal with a fuckwit situation also depends on whether you are an introvert with confidence or a nervous socialiser... nervous socialisers, please walk away.

When having a similar conversation about fuckwits in social situations with one of my coaching clients, she suggested she could very much see me toying with the fuckwit and having a bit of fun.

What do I mean by having fun with them? Basically, remaining in fuckwit territory and annoying the shit out of them by insisting on mingling and conversing with them; being your nicest self and not showing the usual signs of their previous victims.

The fuckwit is expecting the usual reaction of the other person cowering or cow towing. Offer them a different reaction and you have the pleasure of surprising them and swaying their stern, intimidating composure… give me some more of that!

My client's comment demonstrated she knows me well, this makes me happy, I want a good, trusting, long term working relationship with my clients and these comments reassure me that I have been successful in achieving that.

By the way, I don't work with fuckwits, just putting it out there.

I have to admit, this client of mine was spot on. I would have some fun with this situation.

A note of caution here, on days where I feel my energy is not strong enough, I walk away, get myself as far from that negative fuckwit energy as possible and go in search of good energy. Walking away is an inadvertent way of annoying the fuckwit, as you are not giving them the attention they are vying for. You are displaying that you are not looking for their acceptance and are happy in your own skin.

I suggest you do the same if you're not '*feeling*' it. Be patient my friend, wait until you master the skills of socialising before 'toying' with the fuckwits.

It would only be fair to add, at this point, that sometimes fuckwits are scared little children on the inside (at least sometimes). You'll be pleased to know that my 'toying' has on occasion thawed some fuckwits and had them eating out of my hand… oh, the little darlings!

Getting to work

Big Juicy Fruit GEM: Do you want a really quick tip to surviving social events?

Find someone who loves the limelight, they will love talking, they are usually very entertaining and will allow you space to just observe listen and only add the odd bit whenever you choose.

This person will be known from now as the 'Natural Socialiser'.

Once you have the Natural Socialiser on board, get with others and watch this person flow, take charge and whisk you away with them in a flurry of effortless conversation.

A good strategy if you've bought this book a day or two before a social event, a 'quick fix' until you can get down to doing the activities and working through the book.

If you do just that, this book has been a great investment for you, a slightly bias claim on my part. Seriously though, if you didn't have that strategy in your pocket before you read it here, then my claim is valid.

When you are ready to do more and grab just a smidgen of that limelight, you can read the rest.

Before you even start to utilise the other strategies in this short but dynamic book, I need you to ask yourself a few questions. You need to be completely honest with yourself when answering the questions listed.

It's really important that you answer thoroughly, ask yourself if there's more and keep writing until you are no longer able to add to the answer. Answer all the questions in this way throughout the book. My reason for impressing the importance of thorough answers here is because this preliminary question group will set the foundations for the other work ahead.

ACTIVITY:

Honestly and thoroughly answer the questions below:

1. What repels you most about socialising?

2. Where did that belief or feeling come from?

3. If you put it there, what was your reason for putting it there?

4. When did you put it there? This may have been a past experience so think back to when you started feeling this way.

5. If someone else put it there, what makes you continually validate this feeling and keep it in place?

6. On a scale of 1 to 10 how strong is this belief (Scaling: 1 = not at all, 10 = it's got me by the short and curlies, its serious!).

7. You have the power to change that, are you willing to give it a go?

8. If you aren't willing to give it a go, what's stopping you, what's getting in the way? List everything that you feel, believe or recall as a memory.

List

________________ ________________

________________ ________________

________________ ________________

________________ ________________

9. Does that list look as scary as when it was in your head?

GEM: When you write things down it makes it a bit more manageable, some things, when you look at them written down, may no longer feel like a barrier.

Take an objective and honest look at your list.

10. Cross off all that is no longer valid on your list; write down the remaining items on your list here:

_________________   _________________

_________________   _________________

11. How scary or real are those for you? Rate them using the 1 to 10 scaling.

12. Can you think of ways you could make these items less scary?

13. Could you zap some of the remaining items into oblivion, watch them go off into outer space? If you answered YES; DO IT NOW! Close your eyes and watch them being zapped away.

14. How committed are you to work to overcome any remaining items and giving this your very best shot? (circle your answer)

- Slightly
- A bit more than slightly
- I am quite committed
- I am very committed
- Where's the dotted line? I'm ready to sign and fully commit!

If you selected either one of the first two bullet points on question 14, then you're not ready or committed enough to this goal.... go back to the first eight questions and dig deeper, answer them more fully, be totally honest even if it makes you feel a little vulnerable, that's ok we are humans, we all have moments of vulnerability.

Now you have established the reasons for this barrier to socialising and are still committed to making this happen for you. Let's move on.

Are Your Nerves Getting on Your Nerves?

When we are nervous or not quite happy about being somewhere, we tend to start creating noise in our minds, this noise could be lots of 'what if' thoughts or thoughts that you could be elsewhere, or perhaps you're wondering how others will perceive you… whatever it is, it blurs your awareness, your vision and ability to make sound judgements.

Spring Clean Your Mind

Spring cleaning your mind is a particularly good exercise if you are the nervous socialiser. Please don't take this as an implication that you have a dirty mind, although you may very well have. We're all guilty of that on occasion; I'm not terribly concerned about those thoughts at the moment.

What I *am* saying is that you may have a cloudy mind; a cloudy mind fills you with doubt, nerves, anxiety.

GEM: Prepare yourself before the event, take a moment to just sit and notice where your thoughts go, are they all over the place? Quiet them down and start looking at each thought clearly. Looking at our thought patterns from a quiet space creates clarity, take all the negative thoughts and try to understand the reason for them, acknowledge them then let them go. If they don't leave willingly, show them out the door.

Going into a situation with negative energy will only attract negative experiences. You want to ensure that you create a positive energy and positive thoughts before you go into this social situation.

Zap That Negative Energy

Feeling Shitty? Here's a quick fix:

GEM: Stand up, raise your arms high, shoulders relaxed, look up, ideally out of a window into the sky, hold this for a minute or two then notice how you feel.

This is a very effective quick fix to create a positive mind and generate positive energy, you can practically do this anywhere… I do! Yes even in public places, those 'in the know' know exactly what I'm doing, others just think I'm yet another strange, slightly absurd Londoner; frowning at their misfortune of bumping into such bizarre people (chuckle).

If you haven't read or listened to Dr Wayne Dyer (a great soul lost) then you really must give it a go, his 'Everyday Wisdom' audio is one of my things to listen to daily on my way to work or when I'm working from home. His lovely voice imparts great wisdom whilst I'm working; I get something new from it daily.

The one thing I want to share with you is what he says about thoughts and feelings.

He used to start his day by saying out loud

"This is my day… nothing and no one is going to ruin it for me" or something very similar to that.

GEM: He also explains:

If our thoughts control our feelings (which they do), then we can control our feelings through our thoughts.

Did you get that?

"If your thoughts control your feelings, then you can control your feelings by changing your thoughts…"

Preferably from negative to positive; positive thoughts will bring positive responses.

A perfect example which I think the universe sent to me so I could share it with you, is my day today… everything that could go wrong, did go wrong.

Warning: **This real life story is a bit of fluff, I think it is useful fluff, I might even go as far as saying it's interesting fluff, but that's a matter of opinion. If you don't like fluff, you can skip to the next topic 'Appearance'**

My phone stopped working this morning and I'm on my way from London to York, so the timing for this dilemma couldn't have been any worse.

I borrow my daughter's hand-me-down phone (as it still has my email apps on it) and give her an even older emergency phone. I still take my now useless phone with me just in case it decides to wake up. Carrying one phone around is usually my top limit, today I have two plus a laptop.

The tube line announced there would be a strike today, they have also significantly reduced tubes on that line to service the stock; a very challenging start to the day and a challenging journey to Kings Cross to catch my train… but I'm still OK "It's OK" all will be fine (my mantra).

So I get to Kings Cross station, after almost having my last breath squeezed out of me on the Victoria line, "**It's OK"** is all I could say to myself. I had just enough breath left in me to tell the huge guy that he was killing me softly with his bag. If he and his huge rucksack continued to push into me, I would most certainly be taking my very last breath.

He was exceedingly apologetic and proceeded to remove his rucksack from his back, not an easy undertaking in an underground carriage that is more tightly packed than a can of sardines. Needless to say he couldn't avoid whacking the back of my head whilst doing it. Not helping the already sorry state of my hair that could be likened to a lion's mane or more realistically, to electrocution (curly hair can really play up).

I try not to drink too much coffee (my body is my temple) but this ordeal really requires a double caffeine hit to make me feel a bit better. A good few moments later, I realise that my e-ticket bar code is on my 'no longer working' phone… I take a big gulp of my caffeine saviour and think "Oh shit!"

Helper lady at the barriers to the trains was anything but helpful; she was horrid; hungry like a wolf, looking for a victim to feed her ego… I became her target… I was still not going to let anything spoil my day… she did get to me though, I hope karma, the universe, God, any higher power (I'm not fussy) sees me right.

I say a few calming affirmations in my head, do the crazy raising my arms in the air thing and look up to the very high ceiling of Kings Cross station... all in the hope that the hothead which resides within me is not provoked enough to come out and wreak havoc... that hothead within doesn't come out very often but when it does I feel like the agitator has won (although they might disagree by the time I'm done with them) and I don't want that. I don't want to feed that side of me as I'm usually filled with regret after the event.

After unhelpful helper lady had finished telling me I should have known my phone was going to stop working, she went on about it... like a broken record; I think she got a bit freaked out with my crazy person, arms in the air stance (hehehe). I finally got through the barrier to my now imminently departing train.

As I hopped on; for some unknown reason (intuition?), I took out and checked non-working phone and it fires up! Yay! Just in time for the ticket inspector, phew! Pop headphones on with Louise Hay (she is very calming), get my laptop out to tell you about this awful ordeal and the day feels fine again… see?

I am not prepared to allow anyone or anything to spoil my day, despite the lorry load of unfortunate events!

***Mind-set:* control your thoughts and your feelings will respond.**

How life pans out for us really is about how we think, our perspective, what we say to ourselves.

Look around you, listen to positive people and make a note of the words they use. Then do the same with those who always have negative connotations to their conversations… their lives will look like they really suck.

The truth is that both the positive and negative person have had some real pants experiences (as we all have) but it's how they have handled those experiences that makes the difference to how they are perceived by others. It also makes a huge difference to how each day pans out for them.

Appearance

In this high-tech world, where everyone's faces are constantly on social media, people feel heavily scrutinised. This can create an unhealthy level of self-consciousness that can have a negative impact on your self-esteem and outward behaviours.

ACTIVITY:

More questions for you to answer honestly:

- How do you feel about your appearance on a scale of 1 to 10? (scaling 1 = I feel shit about how I look so I've given up trying to look good,10 = I'm an irresistible sex bomb, I'm on fire baby!)

- Would you tweak it a little?

- What would you like to tweak?

____

____

- How will tweaking make things better?

____

____

____

- Can you learn to love those bits about you that you scrutinised through a microscope?

- On a scale of 1 to 10 (be honest!) how much does it matter what others think?
  (scaling 1 = I'm constantly freaking out about what others think when they look at me, 10 = I don't give a flying, singing or dancing fuck)

If you scored low on one or more of these, more work needs to be done. However, how you feel about your appearance and how you are perceived by others can be played around with to a certain degree.

Even on days you feel pants about your appearance, take time getting ready for social events, if it helps to be pampered a little (everyone loves a little pampering) then do that; get your hair done, get a manicure, pedicure; whatever it takes to make you feel good.

If you don't have two pennies to rub together and can't pay for the listed services, (I have been there more times than I care to remember and completely empathise) then read on.

GEM: The solution for this very real, no pennies issue is to do a DIY version (not the hair, please don't cut your own hair!). Make it a nice slow relaxed ritual before the event, have a nice long soak in the bath with nice smelly stuff that is also good for you (and the environment if at all possible), style your hair, give yourself a manicure/pedicure, take time picking your outfit and accessories. This slow pamper process will lift your spirits, refreshing you and your mind-set.

Strut Your Stuff

Take time over getting ready for work, social events or just going out to the supermarket. I know there will be times you can't really be bothered when it's just the supermarket or the corner shop, I will be the first to put my hands up and say I've worn my pyjamas in public on several occasions.

What you need to know is that taking time and getting properly dressed for things is work towards you having an improved self- image. It's you building on and growing your self-esteem; small steps towards a bigger goal.

Do you envy those people who look bloody fantastic daily? I do, in a nice admiring way, not in a bloody hate them way. I don't always take as much time getting ready most days; I love my jeans so very much, I have a wardrobe full of them. I don't feel pants on the days I wear my beloved jeans (which is most days) but I could probably do a bit more with it, you know I could 'rock' that look a bit more than I do.

I have noticed however, the days where I'm off to a meeting, to deliver coaching or training, I take a bit more time getting ready and I have to say, I look 'hot' on those days and I know it, I am totally rocking on those days! Knowing I have taken pride in my appearance is good for my mind and makes me feel so damn fine, my girls' reaction just feeds that 'looking fine' feeling even more... I like that feeling, you will too.

I look at my youngest with great admiration, she is one of those individuals who manage to look fabulous daily; she takes time choosing her outfit for the day and thinks carefully about the accessories, how she'll wear her hair and how she'll do her make-up... down to the finest detail. Oh, I must also add, she is 17 so the make-up is permitted (although I'd prefer she didn't ruin her beautiful flawless skin).

Most days, I really don't have the time or inclination, you may also be thinking the same, but when I see her, I tell myself I should take a leaf out of her book. I know how fine and uplifted I feel when I do take some time over my appearance. It's like an energy booster injection, injecting a new fresh energy directly into your soul and psyche.

Make-up, hair appointments, and designer clothes aren't my point here, I don't want you thinking this is about the shallow image thing… it isn't. However, investing some time on your appearance, giving yourself some TLC can do wonders for you, it will boost your confidence levels which will be reflected outwardly; you'll notice that people react and respond to you differently.

GEM: *Loving yourself is a good thing; arrogance is not a good thing.*

If you're looking to increase your levels of confidence, this is one of the quickest and surest ways of putting a foot (or a leap, in some cases) in the right direction.

ACTIVITY:

What will you do differently now to boost your outward presentation; to boost your soul and psyche?

Write down one, *just one* thing you will do immediately to love yourself and your appearance that little bit more:

I will…………………………………………

…………………………………………………

This new action will be completed on:

Date: ***Time:***

Now write down one thing you will do daily from now on to love your appearance that little bit more:

My daily gift to my appearance will be…

…………………………………………………

…………………………………………………

Confidence

Would it surprise you if I told you that the majority of the people I speak to feel they don't have enough or any confidence? It's quite an eye opener.

A recent statistic reported that 60% of adults are ashamed of the way they look. I wholeheartedly believe that this statistic boils down to confidence and self-esteem, the blasted media images and unrealistic societal expectations don't help the matter much.

Although this isn't the book on confidence I want to spend some time on this topic, you see, I whole-heartedly believe that confidence and self-esteem can be attained... I have had the privilege of seeing so many of my clients turn into amazing, confident people just by working towards and achieving their dreams. It's a wonderful, heart-warming thing to see and be a part of.

Confidence is one of the things that separates the successful people from everyone else. If you spoke to these people they will tell you their confidence levels fluctuate, they are after all, only human. I believe how they handle this fluctuation is what makes them successful.

They know how to overcome doubt, fear, anxiety and they know how to use these nerves by turning them into a positive energy that benefits them in the situation they are facing and applies to social situations too.

In Neuro-linguistic programming (NLP), there is a belief that everyone has the resources they need within them to achieve their desired change.

You have to trust that you have the skills, knowledge and resources you need to achieve the level of confidence you want.

Doubt is just lack of confidence presenting itself in a different way; doubt will lead to all sorts of thoughts in your mind (negative noise). Don't listen to doubt, doubt is a liar.

Doubt is also a sign that you don't trust yourself… if you don't trust yourself, why would others want to place trust in you?

I read a very effective saying somewhere:

"Self-doubt is responsible for killing more dreams than failure ever will"

GEM: Remember that little statement when you are about to allow self-doubt to talk you into a 'tizzy' about a social event.

When you gain confidence and truly believe and trust in yourself, you will be surprised at how easily you can do what you need to do, and how much more enjoyable it is than you had originally thought!

The fear of the unchartered territory, not knowing what you will find is a real barrier for some. If you are a nervous socialiser, this feeling may be magnified.

Fear is an effective barrier for many, stopping them in their tracks, they end up 'not doing' a great deal of things.

Going into what is your unchartered territory can be very daunting... especially if you are in it alone with no one holding your hand, encouraging you forward on this new, exciting and slightly nerve racking adventure.

How you perceive it is going to be the most powerful factor in determining how you embark on your new experience… or whether you embark on it at all.

It is natural to be anxious about the unknown, doing something that you have never done before, coming out of your comfort zone.

Confidence is about you stepping out of your comfort zone… creating a new one and doing it all over again.

Here's a little more meaningful fluff:

One person I truly admire for stepping out of her comfort zone time and time again is my eldest daughter. She is incredible. She was 14 years old when her school offered her the spare place to a trip to Brussels to talk at the EU.

When she came home to tell me this I could see she was both excited and nervous, she was travelling alone, well, without me, at the age of 14, that's as good as alone. She would be away for almost a week; she would not be with her class but with teens two years above her, she knew no one.

Off she went with her school to Brussels, my first experience of letting go, I felt anxiety and pride all at the same time.

When she got to Brussels, she discovered that there were two more girls from her year who were also there, she didn't know them but she felt a bit better.

When picking rooms, my wonderful angel thought that sharing with the girls from her year would be the natural thing… oh no Siree! These girls were fuckwits! They clearly told her she was not welcome; being who she is, this did not sway her enough to impact her confidence.

Moving on, she explored other possibilities. A group of three older girls invited her to share with them and so began a new friendship. My first-born had the time of her life! She even won the award for… wait for it… Social Butterfly!

She went again the following year and has not stopped globetrotting since.

This is the most admirable and extreme example of what it is to step out of your comfort zone. Being as confident as I am I'm not sure how I would have dealt with that situation at 14 years of age.

GEM: Imagine what you have missed and may still miss by allowing doubt, nerves, lack of confidence win by staying in your comfort zone. Now imagine where you could be if you were to take that one brave step… imagine it now, picture it in your head and *believe* that you can.

ACTIVITY:

This book is full of questions; I am after all, a coach and NLP practitioner. Questions are a great way of discovering the inner most blockages to your achieving the things you want to be, do, have.

My intention is not to focus on the fact that you lack confidence, none of us lack confidence in ***every*** aspect of our lives, just some aspects; if socialising is one aspect where your confidence needs a boost, this activity will help.

I want you to go deep inside your own mind and try to find the *root of the low confidence*. By finding the root cause you can deal with it more effectively. Spend as much time as you need on each question.

1. Where did it come from?

____

2. Can you take yourself back to a particular time that affected your confidence in this area?

3. What is making you hold onto that feeling to this day?

____

____

4. If you had to, could you start to look at that experience in a different way to help ease the impact it had on you?

5. If you can't reduce the impact, are you brave enough to give it a go and work around, below, over or under the issue in order to start increasing your confidence?

6. Think about what you ***can*** do to start working to increase your confidence in this area... think small steps; take too big a leap and you may lose the ***will.*** Write down what you can do below:

I can ______________________________

I can ______________________________

I can ______________________________

You only have three 'I cans' because I uphold that small, manageable steps is the way to success.

Writing down what you can do makes things feel almost immediately do-able; the challenge now lies in doing them. So pick two, any two of the things you have said you can do, these by the way, are usually known as goals and actions.

Write down any resources, support or help you need in order to achieve each one. Write down where and when you will find the resources, support or help. At the end of that information, I want you to write down a date and time that you will have achieved this by... go on then, I need you to do that right now.

I Will	**Resources**	**Date & Time**
	When: Where: Who:	
	When: Where: Who:	

Do you know what's really great about all this stuff? You can change this issue you are currently facing and become more confident. This book holds just a few of the secrets to increasing your confidence; it's a mini confidence power bar.

Affirmative

Here are the bits you might consider crazy but they work and neuroscience now also suggests it works, aha!

Start using daily affirmations... say them often enough and your unconscious mind will store the ones that are important for you.

As you absorb these positive affirmative thoughts by repetition, you will begin to believe them. Once these affirmations become stored in your unconscious mind, they become what you believe; believe them and you will behave in that way, behave in that way and you will become. By becoming, you will feel a positive energy; feel that positive energy and you will emit that outwardly.

Achieve that, and you will attract positive energy that is a sure sign that you have achieved a gigantic leap towards confidence. I will even go as far as saying you have achieved a level of self-love that will draw others towards you or make them envy your confidence in yourself.

ACTIVITY:

I'd like you to sit in a quiet place and write down three to four affirmations about your appearance, we all know that what we think about our appearance has a great deal to do with how confident we feel.

Here are a couple to start you off; if you choose to use these, I recommend that you switch or add new words to make the affirmation yours... your mind will respond to your own words, not my words.

Example affirmations:

"I always look well presented"

"I radiate confidence"

Now write yours:

I am….

I…

I…

I…

Don't under estimate the power of the words "I am…"

GEM: Write your affirmations on post it notes and pop them where you will see them daily, preferably first thing in the morning. Say your affirmations out loud three times. Say them often enough and you'll be able to remember them and say them to yourself over the course of your day.

One of my loyal clients has popped a small variety of his own affirmations around his bedroom mirror so when he's getting ready he chooses one or two to read out loud, the difference is clear in the way he now carries himself and deals with life's dilemmas.

You don't have to have all of yours around your bedroom mirror, choose the one that's most appropriate, you can pop the others elsewhere, on the fridge, the cupboard door that holds your favourite mug for your cuppa every morning, the inside of the front door so you get a boost just as you're about to leave the house. Mostly, just *write* them, *use* them, *do it*; that is the crucial part of this confidence building technique. Action is a crucial part of anything you want to succeed at.

Consistently using positive affirmations will make negative beliefs around this area of your life slowly disappear. It's all about neurology my dear. If you want to know how this happens, drop me a line, I like curious people.

Reminder: Control your thoughts and you control your feelings.

This type of approach for some is difficult to digest as something that really works; it's the crazy shit I mentioned in my forward, the part where I mentioned the white jacket? The only way you'll find out whether this mumbo jumbo, airy fairy, one sandwich short of a picnic approach works, is by whole heartedly giving it a go... have the *will* to try it out and see it in action.

This is not magic, you really have to believe what you say for it to work; you have to have the *will* to make the change happen through your affirmations *and* your actions. Willingness is the key to successfully accomplishing most things.

Be willing and act as if

Action is another crucial ingredient to every goal you will ever set yourself.

GEM: In NLP it is believed that if you 'act as if' then you will eventually become; if you feel less confident about your appearance, social competence, abilities than you would like; do all of the above. Act like a person who is full of confidence about their appearance, their social competence, their abilities... practice makes perfect.

The best example of this is to watch people on stage; many famous people look confident and larger than life on stage. However in this world of social media we have news on tap and will read that the reality for some of those famous people is quite different; they aren't as confident as we perceive them to be, they too have anxieties about their image and abilities... but they act 'as if' and they will eventually become. In the meantime we will all perceive them to be confident and larger than life despite what we read, we still see them in the way they want to be perceived through the behaviour they display in the public arena.

Does what others think of you get to you more than it should? I have a great way of dealing with this particular ailment.

If you are going to worry about what others think… you will never get anything done!

ACTIVITY:

Firstly, ask yourself these questions, score the scaling questions from 1 to 10: 1 being very little and 10 being very much...

- How much does their opinion matter to me? Score:

- If it matters a lot, what are the reasons for this?

- How much will their opinion make a difference to any aspect of my life? Score:

Write down all the possible scenarios, yes the ones that have taken residence in your head, and look at them…

Once you've studied your typical scenarios ask yourself these questions (remember, questions are a good way of getting to the bottom of things)

- Is what others think about me more important than my desire to achieve, enjoy and be my wonderful self?

- Will any of the scenarios I create in my head actually happen if I ignore their views and opinions and go ahead anyway?

- If these scenarios do happen, what will the impact be?

____

____

____

____

- How much will the impact affect me? (Scaling:1 = blaahhh! What impact? 10 = serious impact, I'm shitting in my pants)

If that final question scores 10 or goes off the scale this area will need more work and this book is a quickie, so to speak.

I would suggest you work through all the scores of 7 and above as best you can by identifying the reason for scoring so highly. List everything that comes to mind (lists are good, make lists). If you are unable to work through one or two high scoring things, you need a coach!

If you really want to work through the more difficult scores… you need a coach!

Once you have worked through the list, you may find that you have done enough digging and soul work to give less of a shit about others and that's good, no, it's more than just good; it's bloody fabtastic, stupendous, wonderful!

Don't give too much of your time and mind to worrying about what others think, if they think 'arsey' thoughts about you that's their issue, not yours.

Your job is to stick two fingers at them (or one if you prefer) and start practicing strutting your stuff, no better time than the present!

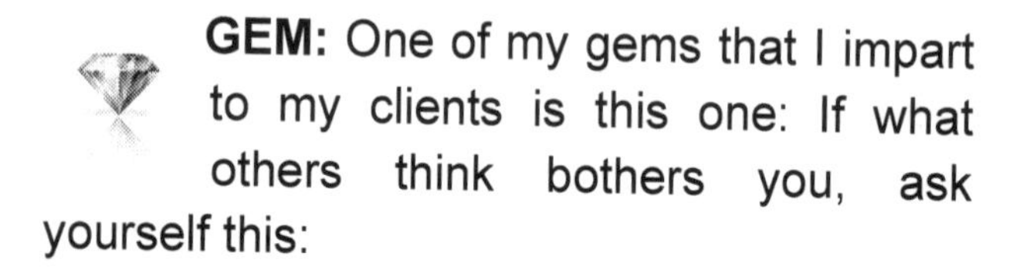

GEM: One of my gems that I impart to my clients is this one: If what others think bothers you, ask yourself this:

Do they positively affect any aspect of my life?

Are they ever going to make a positive contribution to my life?

What have they done for me to date that makes me consider their opinion?

I think you'll find those three questions usually do enough for you to no longer give a fuck and that, my friend, is a wonderful thing.

Become a Zen Student

Get in the Zone

Each day is a gift, enjoy it, damn it! Relax and take each experience in your natural flow, chill and enjoy.

Yes I know it's sometimes easier said than done, I more than anyone get that, and if you don't know what I mean by that, read my blogs. There are ways to deal with the shit life sometimes shovels in your direction, first and foremost... BREATHE!

Did you know that the majority of us don't breathe correctly? By that I mean we don't breathe in the way that helps our body work to optimum levels.

A calm mind has clarity; a calm mind can help you make sound decisions by weighing things up and by taking a rational approach to challenges and barriers.

Breathing is a great way to just relax your body and mind, by focusing on your breathing you are slowly dissolving any anxiety, stress, nerves you may be feeling at the thought of socialising.

Breathing Right

I hope you don't feel like I'm teaching you to suck eggs, you may already know this technique but I don't want to assume anything… as you know to assume is to make an ASS of U and ME (a golden oldie, I'm showing my age)

Quieten your mind, focus on your breath. Breathe in for three and out for four, in through your nose and out through your mouth. Do this for at least fifteen breaths or more if you can. Focusing on your breathing creates a clear space in your mind, it calms the nerves, it stops the noise I mentioned earlier… all those 'what ifs'.

Get a Cat

Cats are real cool cucumbers, they are Zen masters; by modelling a cat, you can gain their wonderful qualities of not giving too much of a shit about anything, doing what feels right, being comfortable in their skin, present and balanced.

I don't seriously want you to get a cat... unless you had already planned to? In that case get a rescue. A pet is for life and they demand and deserve love and respect; a huge and very rewarding responsibility.

I wasn't a cat person at all until we rescued our first cat and now I cannot even remember what I did without them! Oh Yes, did I mention we got two more after the first... uuhhmmm! (Clearing throat).

Meditation is good too; I couldn't meditate for the life of me, now I can't do without it. It clears my mind and heightens my intuitive powers. De-cluttering the noise of modern life and allowing me to take stock of what is important.

Listen to audios that help you relax, change your perception, create a positive energy such as Louise Hay, Abraham Hicks, Dr Wayne Dyer, Deepak Chopra, Eckhart Toll, Tony Robbins... I love them all! Find one that works for you.

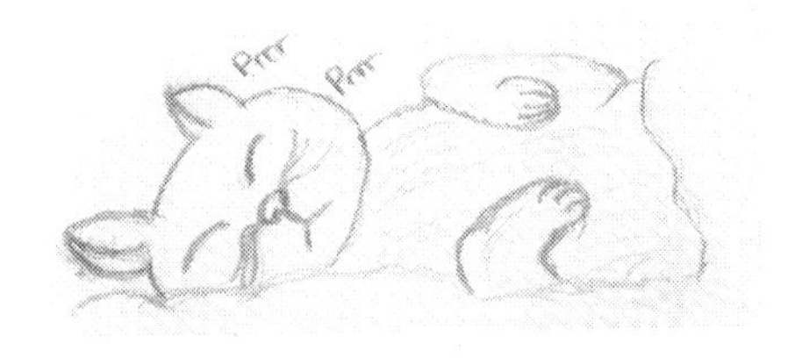

The Secret to 'Minimum Effort' Socialising

If you've read the book to this point, I know you are serious about becoming a social butterfly… or at the very least, being perceived as such!

The fact that you have come thus far tells me the quick fix I gave you earlier isn't what you want and I am so pleased about that.

You see, going through this book and applying the strategies suggested will mean you have invested in your own development.

It tells me you are *willing* to take this journey of personal development and give it your best shot, I'd love to know how you get on so please do drop me an email or post on my FB page, not plugging just genuinely interested in your success.

Now you know how to get your head straight and get in the zone, you need to learn a few simple, minimum effort techniques to socialising and perhaps even enjoying it.

Quick pointers

1. Use your affirmations en route

2. Do your breathing en route.

3. Go in with the mind-set that you are going to enjoy this experience, whatever it brings. As the late and wonderful Dr Wayne Dyer says "Nothing is going to ruin my day, this is my day and nothing and no one is going to ruin it".

4. Have no expectations of the evening/day/event, this will eradicate any disappointment based on preconceptions.

5. If you like music, put some on full blast whilst you get ready for the event.

6. Better still, shake that booty around the house, it releases happy hormones and gets you in the zone (don't get too sweaty, will you? you have a party to get to).

7. Enter with a smile, not a crazy person smile but an assured and relaxed person kind of smile.

8. Take stock of your environment and watch a few people, look out for the fuckwits

9. There might be someone there that looks interesting. If you know the host, get them to introduce you to the one or two people whose energy you like, and there's your starting point.

10. Use your new skills and remember to mingle, don't stay in one place for too long, the key is to sense when conversation is about to run dry... leave before it does.

Hello stranger…

So now you have been introduced, you are expected to make small talk; every introvert's worst nightmare… the ones I know hate small talk, they want juicy and interesting conversations for the time they invest and rightly so!

Luckily, not everyone feels that way so start easy.

Take an Interest

Everyone wants to be made to feel that they are interesting and worthy of being listened to and that's just what you are going to do. What this means for you is minimal talking on your part… isn't that a great start?

Ask questions about what they do. Listen because that's where your clue for the next question will come.

Warning! This is not a Spanish inquisition…

GEM: Asking too many questions in quick succession will make the recipient feel quite uncomfortable. Ask one or two questions and listen to them so you can follow up with a relevant question. Add the odd comment every now and then, so if they say something that resonates with you, comment on it, if they mention something they have done that you have too, comment on it.

Your comment may well lead to the other person continuing talking (great stuff!) if it does lead them to continue, you can continue to flow with questions and comments, if they don't continue after your comment, throw in another relevant question to get the flow going again.

Show you are listening and interested

Have good eye contact, not hypnosis type of eye contact, they'll get freaked out and imagine you living in some dark castle, high up on a hill in a place called Transylvania.

Everything in moderation; if you maintain your Zen composure, smile; all this will be a piece of wonderfully scrumptious, (with a touch of whipped cream and strawberry) melt in your mouth cake. What? Can't a gluten and lactose intolerant person at least imagine these things?

So here's a simple list for you, in no particular order as hopefully you'll do all of it in flow:

- Smile
- Ask questions
- Nod
- Maintain good (not intense) eye contact
- Comment (the odd one every now and then helps)
- Laugh if they say something they think is funny (even if you don't)

Don't stay with one person or group for too long. When you sense the conversation is going dry, excuse yourself and go and mingle elsewhere.

If you are a nervous socialiser, give yourself short breathers in between, get away... go outside for some fresh air or lock yourself in the loo to just breath, raise your arms, look up, recharge.

I know I have already reassured you that these techniques work, but let me endorse that one more time... this shit really works!

Apply Some NLP. NLP is good.

Now to the bits you will most certainly need to practice. Consistency and lots of practice will make you so good at this; you won't even need to think about it after some time (in NLP, we call this unconscious competence).

Are you REALLY listening?

So you're listening, nodding, smiling and asking the odd question, perhaps even making the odd comment.

What do you hear?

What type of words are they using?

Use their words back to them.

So if they say "I ***feel*** like we've met", you don't say "what makes you 'think' that?"

You say "what makes you ***feel*** that?"

It helps build rapport easily and quickly.

Become a Body Buff

No I haven't mixed my words, I don't mean become a buff body (although you may want that too, or perhaps you already are a buff body?)

Let me explain:

We hear so much about how our body language gives out clues to our state of mind or what we are thinking at any given time. It is body language that warns you about the fuckwits when you first meet them. Body language can tell you whether a person is relaxed, nervous, confident, self-conscious, unfriendly, angry, irritated… you get the gist.

How does this help you?

Well I'll tell you. You are going to get a quick, short, sharp lesson in reading and displaying body language to help you in a social context. This whole book is a short sharp lesson; I don't want it to drag on, you might get bored and switch off… where would that leave us? Well, it would leave this book having not completed its fundamental mission and I can't have that! However, this part is crucial to your winning at socialising with minimal effort.

Use Their Body to Take Notes

Please don't scribble on your subject's body; you are just observing, put the markers away.

You may already have instinctively picked up some signs when you were introduced, take note of your instinct, it is there to give you a heads up. Now you need to do a little bit more.

Observe your social target (gosh that sounds so sterile). What are they doing with their hands, arms, legs, feet, body during your first few moments of conversation? Notice and mentally record. Try not to judge what their body language tells you, just observe and make note, you'll need it for the next step.

Use Your Body to Make Friends

Not in the sexual way (unless you want to of course), I mean in the NLP way; building rapport through body language.

Once you have noted your new friend's body language, you need to mirror it. Subtlety is essential in this approach; less is more.

You want to subtly match them, there is a very fine line between making rapport and breaking rapport and with this technique you are right on that line, so be careful.

Overdo it and that person will walk away, either thinking you are a few marbles short or that you were mimicking them in a bid to ridicule them… either of those will leave you being perceived in a negative light. Even if you don't give a flying fuck about what people think… everyone wants to be thought of positively 80% of the time.

Whilst you are listening and asking the odd question, making the odd comment you can start to mirror some of the body language being displayed.

When your body language is in tune with theirs, you are in a good rapport.

Achieving good rapport is the sign of someone who is good at socialising.

Here is your 'at a glance' guide, this is the bit I imagine you may find yourself visiting regularly whilst you are developing your 'socialising with ease' skills.

At a glance point of reference

You will see some things repeated on the tables, that's because they are relevant at more than one stage.

Get into the right mind set

1	*Are you ready? Commit to this goal now*	
2	*Action is the only way to success*	
3	*Remember, nothing is going to spoil your day*	
4	*Affirm. Create and use your affirmations daily, as often as possible*	
5	*Pamper yourself from time to time, give yourself some TLC*	
6	*Practice makes perfect, the more you do this, the easier it will get*	
7	*Give it time and keep at it, the social butterfly within you will gracefully and effortlessly emerge*	

8	*Change your thoughts and your feelings will follow*	

Getting ready to rock 'n' roll

1	*Spring clean your mind: find calm, clarity and courage*	
2	*Breathe, meditate, stroke the cat. Relax*	
3	*Take time getting ready for social events*	
4	*Change your thoughts and your feelings will follow*	
5	*Chase your negative thoughts away as soon as you notice them*	
6	*Get the music on whilst you get ready*	
7	*Shake that booty to get you in the mood, release those happy hormones before you set off*	
8	*Make a promise to yourself that you will enjoy the experience*	

9	*Relax, be you, be free*	
10	*No doubts, don't let the doubtful thoughts take over*	

On your journey and at the event

1	*Chase your negative thoughts away as soon as you notice them*	
2	*Mind-set will determine how the event goes for you, so go with the right mind-set*	
3	*If you're in the car, get some music on, relaxing, party, bass and drum whatever you like to listen to for a 'feel good' lift*	
4	*Relax*	
5	*Make a controlled and confident entrance*	
6	*Find a 'Natural Socialiser' to ease you into this new role of yours*	
7	*Have no expectations, just enjoy every moment*	

8	*Avoid Fuckwits at all costs until you emerge as a social butterfly*	
9	*Don't focus on being liked, focus on having a good time*	
10	*Ask questions… don't make it an inquisition*	
11	*Show a genuine interest in the conversation*	
12	*Make the odd comment*	
13	*When you feel a little frazzled, find a quiet space, raise your arms and look up into the sky… it works!*	
14	*Mingle; don't stay in one place too long, you have a whole room of interesting people to meet*	

References

A list of books that I have read more than once, enjoyed and recommend.

1. Everyday Wisdom, *Dr Wayne W. Dyer*
2. 101 Power Thoughts, *Louise Hay*
3. The little book of mindfulness, *Dr Patrizia Collard*
4. The Power of Now, *Eckhart Tolle*
5. How to win friends and influence people, *Dale Carnegie*
6. The 7 Habits of highly effective people, *Stephen R. Covey*
7. The power of habit, *Charles Duhigg*

About the Author

A whimsical character, despite the many troughs and bumps, I am still quite bouncy and robust internally and outwardly, not in the scary way.

A single parent of two daughters I have buckets of ambition, resilience and drive, my girls are my motivation. I feel honoured to live with two beautiful, charming and intelligent young ladies whom I cannot believe I created (with a little help of course).

I am pleased to say that I am a well-respected and highly regarded trainer, coach and NLP practitioner with over 23 years of experience in developing people in a variety of contexts. I don't know where the years have gone but I have enjoyed each one.

Many years ago, I co-founded a charity working with siblings of children with disabilities, which was set up with a group of professionals in 1998, yep that many years ago! Still managing the same project today (once you've got me there's no going back); as the only remaining founder; this project really is my 'labour of love'.

It is my passion and belief that everyone can be and do anything they put their mind to. My mission is to make a living by doing what I love most; helping as many people reach their full potential before I leave this delightful world. I actually did leave this world once but the good old crash trolley brought me back (a story for another book).

My message to you is the golden thread that runs through this book and the entire pocket coach series: Believe, plan, do, if you stick at it my friend, the world will become your oyster.

If you want to find out more about me join me on:

Facebook:
www.facebook.com/clarityandmotivation/
Twitter:
www.twitter.com/Shahilla1
Instagram:
www.instagram.com/shahilla1/

Resources

You can get access to some free resources on my website: www.shahillabarok.com

A weekly rendezvous with me can be achieved by subscribing to my weekly motivator email programme.

Get yourself a coach if you want to take a serious, sleeves up, ready to do anything stance towards achieving your dreams, goals and aspirations

Join my membership programme and get a full 6-week course as a starter, other courses and resources, and a live weekly coaching session. For more details on this diamond opportunity email me: shahilla@shahillabarok.com

Published by
www.publishandprint.co.uk

32804987R00061

Printed in Great Britain
by Amazon